Congressional Research Service

Brief Summaries of Federal Animal Protection Statutes

Vivian S. Chu
Legislative Attorney

February 1, 2010

Congressional Research Service

7-5700

www.crs.gov

94-731

CRS Report for Congress
Prepared for Members and Committees of Congress

Summary

This report contains brief summaries of federal animal protection statutes, listed alphabetically. It includes statutes enacted to implement certain treaties, but it does not include treaties. Additionally, this report includes statutes that concern animals but that are not necessarily animal protection statutes. For example, it discusses a statute authorizing the eradication of predators, because one of the statute's purposes is to protect domestic and "game" animals; and it includes statutes to conserve fish even though the ultimate purpose of such statutes may not be for the benefit of the fish. This report also includes statutes that allow the disabled to use service animals and statutes aimed at acts of animal rights advocates—i.e., the Animal Enterprise Protection Act of 1992, and the Recreational Hunting Safety and Preservation Act of 1994.

Contents

Contacts

Adoption of Military Animals, 10 U.S.C. § 2583

This statute provides, in part: "The Secretary of the military department concerned may make a military animal of such military department available for adoption ... under circumstances as follows: (1) At the end of the animal's useful life. (2) Before the end of the animal's useful life, if such Secretary ... determines that unusual or extraordinary circumstances justify [it]. (3) When the animal is otherwise excess to the needs of such military department." The statute defines "military animal" as "[a] military working dog" or "[a] horse owned by the Department of Defense." When this statute was first enacted in 2000, it applied only to military working dogs; prior to then, under Department of Defense policy, such dogs were caged, sometimes for as long as a year, and then euthanized. See 146 Cong. Rec. H 9599 (daily ed. October 10, 2000). The statute was amended to cover horses in 2006.[1]

African Elephant Conservation Act, 16 U.S.C. §§ 4201-4245

This statute establishes an African Elephant Conservation Fund, from which the Secretary of the Interior may provide financial assistance "for approved projects for research, conservation, management, or protection of African elephants." It requires the Secretary to establish a moratorium on the importation of raw and worked ivory from an ivory producing country that does not meet specified criteria, including being a party to CITES and adhering to the CITES Ivory Control System. ("CITES" is the Convention on the International Trade in Endangered Species of Wild Fauna and Flora.)

The act imposes civil and criminal penalties on any person who, among other things, imports raw ivory from any country other than an ivory producing country, or from a country for which a moratorium is in effect, or who exports raw ivory from the United States. A person who furnishes information that leads to a civil penalty or a criminal conviction under the act may be rewarded up to one-half of any criminal or civil penalty or fine, or $25,000, whichever is less.

Agriculture Appropriations Act, 2006, P.L. 109-97 (2005), and subsequent appropriations acts

Section 794 of P.L. 109-97 (2005) provides:

> Effective 120 days after the date of enactment of this act, none of the funds made available by this act may be used to pay the salaries or expenses of personnel to inspect horses under section 3 of the Federal Meat Inspection Act (21 U.S.C. 603) or under guidelines issued

---

[1] A comparable provision, P.L. 110-329, § 528, 122 Stat. 3686 (2008), states, "None of the funds made available in this Act may be used to destroy or put out to pasture any horse or other equine belonging to the Federal Government that has become unfit for service, unless the trainer or handler is first given the option to take possession of the equine through an adoption program that has safeguards against slaughter and inhumane treatment."

under section 903 [of] the Federal Agriculture Improvement and Reform Act of 1996 (7 U.S.C. 1901 note; P.L. 104-127).[2]

Because the Federal Meat Inspection Act, 21 U.S.C. § 603, requires horses (and specified other mammals) to be inspected before they may be slaughtered for human consumption, § 794 of P.L. 109-97, by precluding appropriated funds from being used to pay inspectors' salaries and expenses to inspect horses, would have effectively prohibited the slaughter of horses for human consumption from March 10, 2006, until September 30, 2006. The Department of Agriculture, however, on February 8, 2006, issued a regulation allowing slaughter plants to pay for inspections by the Department of Agriculture's Food Safety and Inspection Service so that horses could continue to be slaughtered for human consumption. 9 C.F.R. § 352.19.[3]

The 110th Congress prevented the Department of Agriculture from continuing to charge slaughter plants for inspections, and it thereby effectively prohibited the slaughter of horses for human consumption. It accomplished this by prohibiting appropriated funds from being used not only, as in P.L. 109-97, to pay salaries and expenses under the Federal Meat Inspection Act and the Federal Agriculture Improvement and Reform Act of 1996, but also from being used to implement or enforce 9 C.F.R. § 352.19, under which the Department of Agriculture allowed slaughter plants to pay for inspections. P.L. 110-161, § 741, 121 Stat. 1881 (2007); P.L. 110-329, Div. A, § 101, 122 Stat. 3574-3575 (2008) (incorporating provisions of P.L. 110-161).

Airborne Hunting Act, 16 U.S.C. § 742j-1

This statute makes it a crime (1) while in an aircraft, to shoot any bird, fish, or other animal, or (2) to use an aircraft to harass any bird, fish, or other animal. These prohibitions do not apply to persons employed by or licensed by a state or the federal government to administer or protect "land, water, wildlife, domesticated animals, human life, or crops."

Alaska National Interest Lands Conservation Act

Sections 1313-1314 of this act, 16 U.S.C. §§ 3201-3202, authorize the Secretary of the Interior to designate zones within national preserves in Alaska "where and when no hunting, fishing, trapping, or entry may be permitted," and prohibits "the taking of fish and wildlife" in national parks or national park system monuments in Alaska, except as specified in the act.

Section 1005 of the act, as amended in 1990, 16 U.S.C. § 3145, provides that the Secretary of the Interior

> shall work closely with the State of Alaska and Native Village and Regional Corporations in evaluating the impact of oil and gas exploration, development, production, and transportation and other human activities on the wildlife resources of these lands, including impacts on the

---

[2] Regarding 7 U.S.C. 1901 note, see "Commercial Transportation of Equine for Slaughter," *infra.*

[3] For additional information, see CRS Report RS21842, *Horse Slaughter Prevention Bills and Issues*, by Geoffrey S. Becker. See also Libby Quaid, *Horse Slaughter to Continue Despite Action*, February 7, 2006, at http://www.boston.com/news/nation/washington/articles/2006/02/07/horse_slaughter_to_continue_despite_action/?rss_id=Boston.com%2B/%2BNews.

Arctic and Porcupine caribou herds, polar bears, muskox, grizzly bear, wolf, wolverine, seabirds, shorebirds, and migratory waterfowl.

Americans with Disabilities Act, 42 U.S.C. §§ 12101-12213

This statute (together with the Rehabilitation Act of 1973, 29 U.S.C. §§ 791-794) prohibits discrimination against people with disabilities in employment, public services, and public accommodations.[4] Discrimination includes refusing to make reasonable accommodations for individuals with disabilities, and a reasonable accommodation generally includes permitting the use of service animals, such as seeing eye dogs. See, e.g., 28 C.F.R. § 36.302(c). See also, "Fair Housing Act, 42 U.S.C. § 3604," discussed below.

Anadromous Fish Conservation Act, 16 U.S.C. §§ 757a-757f

This statute authorizes the Secretary of Commerce to take various actions for the protection of fishery resources.

Animal Damage Control Act, 7 U.S.C. §§ 426-426c

This statute directs the Secretary of Agriculture:

> to conduct investigations, experiments, and tests as he may deem necessary in order to determine, demonstrate, and promulgate the best methods of eradication, suppression, or bringing under control on national forests and other areas of the public domain as well as on State, Territory, or privately owned lands of mountain lions, wolves, bobcats, prairie dogs, gophers, ground squirrels, jack rabbits, brown tree snakes, and other animals injurious to agriculture, horticulture, forestry, animal husbandry, wild game animals, fur-bearing animals, and birds.

This statute was enacted in 1931 (though "brown tree snakes" were added in 1991). The functions of the Secretary of Agriculture under it were transferred to the Secretary of Interior in 1939, and back to Agriculture in 1985.[5] In 1987, P.L. 100-202, 101 Stat. 1329-331, added the following provision to the act:

---

[4] The Rehabilitation Act applies to federal executive branch agencies, federal contractors, and federal programs receiving federal financial assistance. The ADA applies to legislative branch agencies, the states, and the private sector.

[5] The transfer in 1985 did not explicitly appear in any federal statute; rather, P.L. 99-190, § 101(a), incorporated H.Rept. 99-439, and Amendment No. 31 to H.Rept. 99-439 incorporated a Senate amendment that appears at 131 *Cong. Rec.* 27449 (October 15, 1985). These provisions are set forth in "Federal Laws Enacted in 1985 Concerning Animals" (February 19, 1985), a CRS report by the present author. These provisions were declared "effective as if enacted into law" by P.L. 100-202, § 106, 101 Stat. 1329-433 (1987). The 1985 transfer to the Department of Agriculture was, according to the Washington Post (January 2, 1986), "to the delight of western cattlemen and sheep producers and the dismay of conservationists"; the issue is debated at 131 *Cong. Rec.* 27459 (October 15, 1985).

The Secretary of Agriculture is authorized, except for urban rodent control, to conduct activities and enter into agreements with States, local jurisdictions, individuals, and public and private agencies, organizations, and institutions in the control of nuisance mammals and birds and those mammal and bird species that are reservoirs for zoonotic diseases, and to deposit any money collected under any such agreement into the appropriation accounts that incur the costs to be available immediately and to remain available until expended for Animal Damage Control activities.

Animal Disease Risk Assessment, Prevention, and Control Act of 2001, P.L. 107-9 (2001)

This statute requires the Department of Agriculture to submit to the House and Senate agriculture committees a preliminary report by June 23, 2001, and a final report by October 20, 2001, concerning foot-and-mouth disease, bovine spongiform encephalopathy, and related diseases.

Animal Enterprise Terrorism Act, 18 U.S.C. § 43

This statute, which replaced the Animal Enterprise Protection Act of 1992, makes it a crime to "travel[ ] in interstate or foreign commerce, or use[ ] ... the mail or any facility in interstate or foreign commerce—(1) for the purpose of damaging or interfering with the operations of an animal enterprise; and (2) in connection with such purpose—(A) intentionally damag[ing] or caus[ing] the loss of any real or personal property ... [or] (B) intentionally plac[ing] a person in reasonable fear of the death of, or serious bodily injury to that person, a member of the immediate family ... of that person, or a spouse or intimate partner of that person. ..." The statute defines "animal enterprise" as:

> (A) a commercial or academic enterprise that uses or sells animals or animal products for profit, food or fiber production, agriculture, education, research, or testing;
>
> (B) a zoo, aquarium, animal shelter, pet store, breeder, furrier, circus, rodeo, or other lawful competitive animal event; or
>
> (C) any fair or similar event intended to advance agricultural arts and sciences.

Animal Health Protection Act, 7 U.S.C. §§ 8301-8321

This statute authorizes the Secretary of Agriculture, if he determines it to be necessary to prevent the introduction into or dissemination with the United States of any pest or disease of livestock, to prohibit or restrict, among other things, the importation or exportation of any animal into or from the United States, the movement in interstate commerce of any animal, or the use of any means of conveyance in connection with the importation or entry of livestock. The statute also authorizes the Secretary, if it is necessary for the above purpose, to order the destruction or removal from the United States of any animal, or to seize, quarantine, or dispose of any animal.

Animal Welfare Act, 7 U.S.C. §§ 2131-2159

The AWA authorizes the Secretary of Agriculture to "promulgate standards to govern the humane handling, care, treatment, and transportation of animals by dealers, research facilities, and exhibitors."[6] 7 U.S.C. § 2143(a)(1). Such standards must include requirements "for animal care, treatment, and practices in experimental procedures to ensure that animal pain and distress are minimized. ..." 7 U.S.C. § 2143(a)(3)(A). The act also requires the Secretary to "promulgate standards to govern the transportation in commerce, and the handling, care, and treatment in connection therewith, by intermediate handlers, air carriers, or other carriers, of animals consigned by any ... person ... for transportation in commerce." 7 U.S.C. § 2143(a)(4).

The AWA's definition of "animal" makes the act applicable to any warmblooded animal used "for research, testing, experimentation, or exhibition purposes, or as a pet; but such term excludes (1) birds, rats of the genus Rattus, and mice of the genus Mus, bred for use in research, (2) horses not used for research purposes, and (3) other farm animals. ..." 7 U.S.C. § 2132(g). Prior to this provision's amendment by P.L. 107-171 (2002), § 10301, it did not exclude birds, rats, or mice. Nevertheless, the Secretary had promulgated regulations that excluded birds, and rats and mice bred for use in research, from coverage under the act. A federal court found this exclusion to violate the act, but the decision was overturned on appeal on the ground that the plaintiffs lacked standing to bring the suit.[7] Subsequently, in a case unrelated to the birds, rats, and mice question, the en banc D.C. Circuit held that a plaintiff who "suffered [injuries] to his aesthetic interest in observing animals living under humane conditions" had standing to sue the Secretary of Agriculture to enforce the act.[8]

Subsequently, another suit was brought to challenge the exclusion of birds, rats, and mice, and a federal district court, citing the D.C. Circuit case, denied the Department of Agriculture's motion to dismiss for lack of standing.[9] As a result, the Department of Agriculture settled the case by agreeing to revise its regulations to include birds, rats, and mice. Then Congress intervened, and, in the Department of Agriculture appropriations for FY2001 (P.L. 106-387, § 772), prohibited FY2001 funds from being used to "modify the definition of 'animal' in existing regulations pursuant to the Animal Welfare Act." The FY2002 appropriations contained the same prohibition (P.L. 107-76, § 732), and then P.L. 107-171, § 10301, amended the statute to exclude birds, rats, and mice bred for research. Section 10304 of the statute, however, directs the National Research Council, by May 13, 2003, to submit to the House and Senate Agriculture Committees "a report on the implications of including rats, mice, and birds within the definition of animal under the regulations promulgated under the Animal Welfare Act (7 U.S.C. 2131 et seq.)." No report appears to have been written.

The AWA requires every research facility to establish an Institutional Animal Committee of at least three members, at least one of whom shall not be affiliated in any way with the facility and

---

[6] The AWA defines "exhibitor" as "any person ... exhibiting any animals, which were purchased in commerce or ... will affect commerce, ... and such term includes carnivals, circuses, and zoos," but "excludes retail pet stores, ... State and county fairs, livestock shows, rodeos, purebred dog and cat shows, and any other fairs or exhibitions intended to advance agricultural arts and sciences." 7 U.S.C. § 2132(h). The Department of Agriculture added another exclusion: "horse and dog races." 9 C.F.R. § 1.1.

[7] Animal Legal Defense Fund v. Espy, 23 F.3d 496 (D.C. Cir. 1994).

[8] Animal Legal Defense Fund v. Glickman, 154 F.3d 426, 429 (D.C. Cir. 1998), *cert. denied*, 526 U.S. 1064 (1999).

[9] Alternatives Research & Development Foundation v. Glickman, 101 F. Supp. 2d 7 (D.D.C. 2000).

---

who is intended to represent "general community interests in the proper care and treatment of animals." The Committee's responsibilities include to review practices involving pain to animals and to file a report with the Secretary. 7 U.S.C. § 2143(b).

The AWA also provides for the licensing of dealers and exhibitors (7 U.S.C. § 2133) and prohibits research facilities from purchasing dogs or cats from unlicensed dealers or exhibitors (7 U.S.C. § 2137). The act defines "dealer" in part as a person who, for compensation, transports, buys, or sells any animal "for research, teaching, exhibition, or use as a pet," but it excludes from the definition a retail pet store that does not sell "animals to a research facility, an exhibitor, or a dealer" (7 U.S.C. § 2132(f)). The act defines "exhibitor" to include carnivals, circuses, and zoos, but to exclude retail pet stores, state and country fairs, livestock shows, rodeos, and purebred dog and cat shows (7 U.S.C. § 2132(h)).

The AWA also prohibits dealers and exhibitors from selling or otherwise disposing of any dog or cat within five business days after they acquire it, except that this requirement does not apply to operators of auction sales. 7 U.S.C. § 2135. A 1990 amendment requires public and private pounds and shelters, and research facilities licensed by the Department of Agriculture, to "hold and care for" any dog or cat they acquire "for a period of not less than five days to enable such dog or cat to be recovered by its original owner or adopted by other individuals before such entity sells such dog or cat to a dealer."[10] 7 U.S.C. § 2158(a). Does this provision prohibit a pound, shelter, or research facility from euthanizing a dog or cat before five days? Perhaps not on its face, but that appears to be its intent, as to read it otherwise would seem to defeat its purpose.[11]

Another 1990 amendment authorized the Attorney General to seek, and federal courts to issue, injunctions against dealing in stolen animals or placing the health of an animal in serious danger in violation of the act. 7 U.S.C. § 2159.

P.L. 110-234, § 14210 (2008)[12] added a new section to the AWA (7 U.S.C. § 2148) that prohibits any person from importing a dog into the United States for purposes of resale unless the Secretary determines that the dog is in good health, has received all necessary vaccinations, and is at least six months old. This section does not apply, however, if a dog is imported for research purposes or veterinary treatment, or if it is imported into Hawaii from the British Isles, Australia, Guam, or New Zealand, if the dog is not transported out of Hawaii for purposes of resale at less than six months of age. P.L. 110-234, § 14214, also amended the AWA (7 U.S.C. § 2149(b)) to increase, from $2,500 to $10,000, the civil penalty that the Secretary of Agriculture may assess for any violation of any provision of the act, or of any rule, regulation, or standard promulgated by the Secretary.

Animal Fighting, 7 U.S.C. § 2156, 18 U.S.C. § 49

The Animal Welfare Act, as amended, most recently by P.L. 110-234, § 14207 (2008) prohibits any person "to knowingly sponsor or exhibit an animal in an animal fighting venture," or "to

---

[10] A "dealer" is defined to include any person who buys an animal, and therefore could include a research facility. 7 U.S.C. § 2132(f).

[11] The regulations do not address this question. See 9 C.F.R. § 2.133(a).

[12] This section of P.L. 110-234, as well as the other sections of P.L. 110-234 cited in the text below, were also included, with the same section numbers, in P.L. 110-246.

knowingly sell, buy, possess, train, transport, deliver, or receive any animal for the purposes of having the animal participate in an animal fighting venture." However,

> [w]ith respect to fighting ventures involving live birds in a State where it would not be a violation of the law, it shall be unlawful under this subsection for a person to sponsor or exhibit a bird in a fighting venture only if the person knew that any bird in the fighting venture was knowingly bought, sold, delivered, transported, or received in interstate commerce for the purpose of participation in the fighting venture.[13]

On August 15, 2008, a Louisiana statute (14:102.23) took effect that made it the 50th state (plus the District of Columbia) to outlaw cockfighting, thereby essentially rendering moot this exception in the AWA.

P.L. 110-22 (2007) made it "unlawful for any person to knowingly sell, buy, transport, or deliver in interstate or foreign commerce a knife, a gaff, or any other sharp instrument attached, or designed or intended to be attached, to the leg of a bird for use in an animal fighting venture." P.L. 110-22 also increased the penalty for violations of the animal fighting ventures section from a misdemeanor to a felony, with a maximum penalty of a fine and three years' imprisonment per violation. P.L. 110-234, § 14207(b) (2008) then increased the maximum penalty to a fine and five years' imprisonment per violation.

The animal fighting section of the AWA also prohibits knowingly using the mail or any instrumentality of interstate commerce to advertise an animal, or a sharp instrument, for use in an animal fighting venture, or to promote or further an animal fighting venture, except that this prohibition applies "to fighting ventures involving live birds only if the fight is to take place in a State where it would be in violation of the laws thereof."

Antarctic Conservation Act of 1978, 16 U.S.C. §§ 2401-2412

This statute makes it unlawful for any United States citizen, unless authorized by the Director of the National Science Foundation, to engage in commerce in any native animal or native bird taken in Antarctica.

Antarctic Marine Living Resources Convention Act of 1984, 16 U.S.C. §§ 2431-2444

This statute implements the Convention on the Conservation of Antarctic Marine Living Resources, and makes it unlawful to harvest, or knowingly to engage in commerce in any Antarctic marine living resource harvested in violation of the Convention.

---

[13] 7 U.S.C. § 2156(a), as amended by P.L. 107-171, § 10302 (2002); see also 39 U.S.C. § 3001(a). Prior to its 2002 amendment, 7 U.S.C. § 2156(a) did not apply at all to fighting ventures involving live birds in states where such activity was legal.

Asian Elephant Conservation Act of 1997, 16 U.S.C. §§ 4261-4266

This statute establishes the Asian Elephant Conservation Fund and directs the Secretary of the Interior to use amounts in the Fund for projects for the conservation of Asian elephants.

Atlantic Coastal Fisheries Cooperative Management Act, 16 U.S.C. §§ 5101-5108

The statute requires the Secretary of Commerce, in cooperation with the Secretary of the Interior, to develop and implement a program to support the interstate fishery management efforts of the Atlantic States Marine Fisheries Commission.

Atlantic Salmon Convention Act of 1982, 16 U.S.C. §§ 3601-3608

This statute limits salmon fishing pursuant to the Convention for the Conservation of Salmon in the North Atlantic Ocean.

Atlantic Striped Bass Conservation Act, 16 U.S.C. §§ 5151-5158

This statute directs the Secretary of Commerce and the Secretary of the Interior to jointly declare a moratorium on fishing for Atlantic striped bass within the coastal waters of any state that does not comply with the plan for managing Atlantic striped bass that is adopted by the Atlantic States Marine Fisheries Commission.

Atlantic Tunas Convention Act of 1975, 16 U.S.C. §§ 971-971k

This statute authorizes the Secretary of Commerce to promulgate regulations to "limit the size of the fish and the quantity of the catch which may be taken from each area ... [and] limit or prohibit the incidental catch of a regulated species. ..."

Bald and Golden Eagle Protection Act, 16 U.S.C. §§ 668-668d

This statute makes it a crime to possess, buy, sell, or transport any bald or golden eagle, alive or dead, or any part, nest, or egg thereof. The Secretary of the Interior may issue regulations authorizing exceptions "for the scientific or exhibition purposes of public museums, scientific societies, and zoological parks, or for the religious purposes of Indian tribes, or ... for the protection of wildlife or of agricultural or other interests in any particular locality. ..."

Captive Wildlife Safety Act: See Lacey Act Amendments of 1981

Chimpanzee Health Improvement, Maintenance, and Protection Act, 42 U.S.C. § 287a-3a

The CHIMP Act, P.L. 106-551 (2000), as amended by P.L. 110-170 (2007), added § 481C to the Public Health Service Act. It requires the Secretary of Health and Human Services (HHS) to "provide for the establishment and operation ... of a [sanctuary] system to provide for the lifetime care of chimpanzees that have been used, or were bred or purchased for use, in research conducted or supported by the National Institutes of Health, the Food and Drug Administration, or other agencies of the Federal Government," when such "surplus chimpanzees" are not needed for such research. Non-federal chimpanzees may also be accepted into the system. Chimpanzees in the system may not be used in research except as specified in the statute, and must be cared for in accordance with the Animal Welfare Act.

The sanctuary system shall be operated by a nonprofit private entity under a contract awarded by the Secretary of HHS. The nonprofit private entity shall have a board of directors composed of not more than 13 voting members, who shall include individuals with expertise and experience in various fields, including primate veterinary care, animal protection, behavioral primatology, management of nonprofit organizations, laboratory animal medicine, and biohazards.

Commercial Transportation of Equine for Slaughter, 7 U.S.C. § 1901 note

This statute, enacted as part of P.L. 104-127, 110 Stat. 1184 (1996), provides that "the Secretary of Agriculture may issue guidelines for the regulation of the commercial transportation of equine for slaughter by persons regularly engaged in that activity within the United States." Specifically, "the Secretary of Agriculture shall review the food, water, and rest provided to equine for slaughter in transit, the segregation of stallions from other equine during transit, and such other issues as the Secretary considers appropriate." The Secretary's regulations implementing this statute were issued in 2001 and are published at 9 C.F.R. Part 88.[14]

Department of Defense Appropriations Acts

P.L. 101-511, § 8019 (1990) provides:

> None of the funds appropriated by this Act or hereafter shall be used to purchase dogs or cats or otherwise fund the use of dogs or cats for the purpose of training Department of Defense students or other personnel in surgical or other medical treatment of wounds produced by any type of weapon: *Provided*, That the standards of such training with respect to the treatment of animals shall adhere to the Federal Animal Welfare Law and to those prevailing in the civilian medical community.

This provision, without the words "or hereafter," had been included in Department of Defense appropriations statutes since P.L. 98-212, § 791 (1984). However, because of the words "or hereafter" in the language quoted above, this prohibition on the use of funds continues to operate unless it is repealed.

Other Department of Defense appropriations statutes use the phrase "this Act or any other Act" instead of "this Act or hereafter." The Comptroller General has "held that the words 'or any other act' do not indicate futurity, but merely extend the effect of the provisions to other appropriations available in that fiscal year." 65 Comp. Gen. 588, 589 (1986). The following example of the use of this phrase in connection with the use of animals in research appeared in P.L. 103-139, § 8044 (1993), and P.L. 104-61, § 8034 (1995):

> None of the funds provided in this Act or any other Act shall be available to conduct bone trauma research at any Army Research Laboratory until the Secretary of the Army certifies that the synthetic compound to be used in the experiments is of such a type that its use will result in a significant medical finding, the research has military application, the research will be conducted in accordance with the standards set by an animal care and use committee, and the research does not duplicate research already conducted by a manufacturer or any other research organization.[15]

Finally, some limitations on the use of Department of Defense funds for animal research have applied only to a particular appropriations statute. For example, P.L. 103-139 § 8043 (1993), and P.L. 104-61, § 8032 (1995), provide:

> None of the funds appropriated by this Act shall be available for payments under the Department of Defense contract with the Louisiana State University Medical Center involving the use of cats for Brain Missile Wound Research. ...

---

[14] See also "Agriculture Appropriations Act, 2006, P.L. 109-97 (2005), and subsequent appropriations acts," *supra*.

[15] The bone trauma research involves the use of dogs; see H.Rept. 101-345, 101st Cong., 1st sess. 153 (1989).

Departments of Labor, Health and Human Services, and Education, and Related Agencies Appropriations Act for the Fiscal Year Ending September 30, 1993

P.L. 102-394, § 213 (1992) provides:

> No funds appropriated under this Act or subsequent Departments of Labor, Health and Human Services, and Education, and Related Agencies Appropriations Acts shall be used by the National Institutes of Health, or any other Federal agency, or recipient of Federal funds on any project that entails the capture or procurement of chimpanzees obtained from the wild. For purposes of this section, the term "recipient of Federal funds" includes private citizens, corporations, or other research institutions located outside the United States that are recipients of Federal funds.

This provision had previously appeared, without the reference to subsequent acts, in P.L. 101-166, § 214 (1989), P.L. 101-517, § 211 (1990), and P.L. 102-170, § 213 (1991).

Depictions of Animal Cruelty, 18 U.S.C. § 48

This statute, enacted as P.L. 106-152 (1999), makes it a crime knowingly to create, sell, or possess any visual or audio "depiction of animal cruelty with the intention of placing that depiction in interstate or foreign commerce for commercial gain." It provides an exception for "any depiction that has serious religious, political, scientific, educational, journalistic, historical, or artistic value." The statute was aimed at outlawing "crush video" films, in which small animals are crushed to death. A federal court of appeals has held that the statute violates the First Amendment's guarantee of freedom of speech, and the Supreme Court has agreed to review the case. *United States v. Stevens*, 533 F.3d 218 (3d Cir. 2008) (en banc), *cert. granted*, No. 08-769 (Apr. 20, 2009).

Dingell-Johnson Sport Fish Restoration Act, 16 U.S.C. §§ 777-777*l*

This statute is also known as the "Federal Aid in Fish Restoration Act" and the "Fish Restoration and Management Projects Act." It directs the Secretary of the Interior "to cooperate with the States through their respective State fish and game departments in fish restoration and management projects." It includes the New England Fishery Resources Restoration Act of 1990, 16 U.S.C. § 777e-1. This statute was amended by the Wildlife and Sport Fish Restoration Programs Improvement Act of 2000, discussed below.

Disposition of Unfit Horses And Mules, 40 U.S.C. § 1308

This statute provides, in full:

> Subject to applicable regulations under this subtitle and title III of the Federal Property and Administrative Services Act of 1949 (41 U.S.C. 251 et seq.), horses and mules belonging to the Federal Government that have become unfit for service may be destroyed or put out to pasture, either on pastures belonging to the Government or those belonging to financially sound and reputable humane organizations whose facilities permit them to care for the horses and mules during the remainder of their natural lives, at no cost to the Government.

Dog and Cat Protection Act of 2000, 19 U.S.C. § 1308

This statute, P.L. 106-476, §§ 1441-1443 (2000), makes it unlawful to import into, or export from, the United States any dog or cat fur product; or to engage in interstate commerce in any dog or cat fur product.

Dolphin Protection Consumer Information Act, 16 U.S.C. § 1385

This statute, as amended by § 5 of the International Dolphin Conservation Program Act, P.L. 105-42 (1997), makes it a violation of § 5 of the Federal Trade Commission Act, 15 U.S.C. § 45,

> for any producer, importer, exporter, distributor, or seller of any tuna product that is exported from or offered for sale in the United States to include on the label of that product the term "dolphin safe" or any other term or symbol that falsely claims or suggests that the tuna contained in the product were harvested using a method of fishing that is not harmful to dolphins if the product contains tuna harvested—
>
> (A) on the high seas by a vessel engaged in driftnet fishing; or
>
> (B) outside the eastern tropical Pacific Ocean by a vessel using purse seine nets ...
>
> (C) in the eastern tropical Pacific Ocean by a vessel using a purse seine net unless the tuna meet the requirements for being considered dolphin safe under paragraph (2). ...

Violators are subject to a civil penalty of up to $100,000.

Driftnet Impact Monitoring, Assessment, and Control Act of 1987, 16 U.S.C. § 1822 note

This statute finds that "the use of long plastic driftnets is a fishing technique that may result in the entanglement and death of enormous numbers of target and nontarget marine resources in the waters of the North Pacific Ocean, including the Bering Sea." It therefore provides that the Secretary of Commerce, through the Secretary of State, shall negotiate with foreign governments to monitor driftnet fishing, and shall evaluate the feasibility of various methods of reducing the number of driftnets discarded or lost at sea.

The Driftnet Act Amendments of 1990, 16 U.S.C. § 1826, incorporate and expand upon provisions of the Driftnet Impact Monitoring, Assessment, and Control Act of 1987.

Eastern Pacific Tuna Licensing Act of 1984, 16 U.S.C. §§ 972-972h

This statute makes it unlawful to fish for designated species of tuna within the "Area Agreement" specified in the act without a license, or in contravention of regulations promulgated by the Secretary of Commerce.

Endangered Species Act, 16 U.S.C. §§ 1531-1544

This statute authorizes the Secretary of the Interior (the Secretary of Commerce in the case of marine mammals) to promulgate lists of species which are endangered or threatened (defined as "likely to become ... endangered") and to designate critical habitats of such species. Among other things, the act prohibits any person or private or governmental entity from importing, exporting, taking, possessing, selling, or transporting any endangered species. 16 U.S.C. § 1538. It prohibits federal agencies, unless granted an exemption, from taking action "likely to jeopardize the continued existence of any endangered species or threatened species or result in the destruction or adverse modification of [critical] habitat of such species." 16 U.S.C. § 1536(a)(2). (No similar prohibition applies to entities other than federal agencies.) The act also requires the Secretary to develop and implement recovery plans for the conservation and survival of endangered and threatened species. 16 U.S.C. § 1533(f).

In 1988, P.L. 100-478 amended the act to require the Secretary to develop and implement recovery plans for the conservation and survival of endangered species and threatened species, and to implement a system in cooperation with the states to monitor the status of recovered species. It also directed the Secretary of Commerce to contract for an independent review, by the National Academy of Sciences, of scientific information pertaining to the conservation of sea turtles.

Fair Housing Act, 42 U.S.C. § 3604

This statute, as interpreted by the Department of Housing and Urban Development (HUD), requires that all public and private housing (except as exempted in 42 U.S.C. §§ 3603(b) and § 3607) allow seeing eye dogs, even if they otherwise have a "no pets" policy. 24 C.F.R. § 100.204. The act prohibits discrimination "in the terms, conditions, or privileges of sale or rental of a dwelling, or in the provision of services or facilities in connection" with such a dwelling, because of a race, color, religion, sex, familial status (living with children), national origin, or handicap. One form of discrimination based on handicap is "a refusal to make reasonable accommodations in rules, policies, practices, or services, when such accommodations may to necessary to afford [a handicapped] person equal opportunity to use and enjoy a dwelling." HUD has determined that allowing seeing eye dogs is a reasonable accommodation.

Federal Hazardous Substances Act, 15 U.S.C. §§ 1261-1275

The Consumer Product Safety Commission, which administers this statute, adopted a policy statement on animal testing "intended to minimize the number of animals tested and to reduce the pain associated with such tests." The statement notes "that neither the FHSA nor the Commission's regulations require any firm to perform animal tests," although it adds that "animal testing may be necessary in some cases." 49 *Fed. Reg.* 22522 (May 30, 1984).

Federal Law Enforcement Animal Protection Act of 2000, 18 U.S.C. § 1368

This statute makes it a crime "willfully and maliciously" to harm a dog or horse used by a federal agency in law enforcement.

Fish and Wildlife Conservation Act, 16 U.S.C. §§ 2901-2912

This statute authorizes the Secretary of the Interior to approve state conservation plans for "nongame fish and wildlife," which are defined as "wild vertebrate animals that are in an unconfined state and that—(A) are not ordinarily taken for sport, fur, or food ...; (B) are not listed as endangered species or threatened species ... and (C) are not marine mammals. ..." A 1988 amendment (adding 16 U.S.C. § 2912) requires the Secretary to undertake research and conservation activities concerning population trends of, and the effects of environmental changes and human activities on, "migratory nongame birds."

Fish And Wildlife Coordination Act, 16 U.S.C. §§ 661-667d

This statute authorizes the Secretary of the Interior:

> to provide assistance to, and cooperate with, Federal, State, and public or private agencies and organizations in the development, protection, rearing, and stocking of all species of wildlife, resources thereof, and their habitat, and in controlling losses of the same from disease or other causes, in minimizing damages from overabundant species, in providing public shooting and fishing areas. ...

Fishery Conservation Amendments of 1990, P.L. 101-627

In addition to containing numerous amendments of the Magnuson Fishery Conservation and Management Act and the Atlantic Tunas Convention Act of 1975, this statute includes the Dolphin Protection Consumer Information Act, which this report summarizes separately.

Food, Agriculture, Conservation, and Trade Act of 1990, 7 U.S.C. § 5801(a)(5)

This statute funds "research designed to increase our knowledge concerning agricultural production systems that" serve six specified purposes, one of which is to "promote the well being of animals."

Fur Seal Act of 1966, 16 U.S.C. §§ 1151-1175

This statute prohibits the "taking" (defined as to "harass, hunt, capture, or kill") of fur seals in the North Pacific Ocean or on any lands or waters under the jurisdiction of the United States, or to engage in commerce in fur seals' skins taken contrary to the act or the Interim Convention on the Conservation of North Pacific Fur Seals.

The act contains an exception allowing taking by "Indians, Aleuts, and Eskimos who dwell on the coasts of the North Pacific Ocean," and authorizes the Secretary of Commerce to permit taking for "educational, scientific, or exhibition purposes." The act also directs the Secretary to administer the fur seal rookeries on the Pribilof Islands to "ensure that activities on such Islands are consistent with the purposes of conserving, managing, and protecting the North Pacific fur seals and other wildlife. ..." The 1983 amendments to the act repealed the Protection of Sea Otters on the High Seas Act, formerly 16 U.S.C. §§ 1171-1172, as unnecessary because of the enactment of the Marine Mammal Protection Act of 1972.

Great Ape Conservation Act of 2000, 16 U.S.C. §§ 6301-6305

This statute "established in the Multinational Species Conservation Fund a separate account to be known as the 'Great Ape Conservation Fund.'" The Secretary of the Interior shall use the fund for projects that he approves for the conservation of great apes.

High Seas Fishing Compliance Act of 1995, 16 U.S.C. §§ 5501-5509

The purpose of this statute is "(1) to implement the Agreement to Promote Compliance with International Conservation and Management Measures by Fishing Vessels on the High Seas ... , and (2) to establish a system of permitting, reporting, and regulation for vessels of the United States fishing on the high seas."

Horse Protection Act, 15 U.S.C. §§ 1821-1831

This statute makes it a crime to exhibit, or transport for the purpose of exhibition, any "sore" horse, which is a horse whose feet have been injured in order to alter the horse's gait. The Secretary of Agriculture is authorized to enforce the act.

The Horse Protection Act also provides that "no horse may be exported by sea from the United States, or any of its territories or possessions, unless such horse is part of a consignment of horses with respect to which a waiver has been granted" by the Secretary of Commerce. Such waivers may be granted only "if the Secretary of Commerce, in consultation with the Secretary of Agriculture, determines that no horse in that consignment is being exported for purposes of slaughter."[16]

Humane Slaughter Act, 7 U.S.C. §§ 1901-1906

The central provision of the Humane Slaughter Act (HSA) reads:

> No method of slaughter or handling in connection with slaughtering shall be deemed to comply with the public policy of the United States unless it is humane. Either of the following two methods of slaughtering and handling are hereby found to be humane:
>
> (a) in the case of cattle, calves, horses, mules, sheep, swine, and other livestock, all animals are rendered insensible to pain by a single blow or gunshot or an electrical, chemical or other means that is rapid and effective, before being shackled, hoisted, thrown, cast, or cut; or
>
> (b) by slaughtering in accordance with the ritual requirements of the Jewish faith or any other religious faith that prescribes a method of slaughter whereby the animal suffers loss of consciousness by anemia of the brain caused by the simultaneous and instantaneous severance of the carotid arteries with a sharp instrument and handling in connection with such slaughtering.

---

[16] 18 U.S.C. § 1824a. This section was originally enacted as part of the Export Administration Amendments Act of 1985, P.L. 99-64, and was codified at 46 U.S.C. App. § 466. In addition, P.L. 107-171, § 10418(a)(2) (2002), repealed 42 U.S.C. §§ 3901-3902, which had authorized the Secretary of Agriculture to "prescribe regulations governing accommodations on board vessels for cattle, horses, mules, asses, sheep, goats, and swine to be carried from the United States to a foreign country. The regulations shall prescribe standards for space, ventilation, fittings, food and water supply, and other requirements the Secretary of Agriculture considers necessary for the safe and proper transportation and humane treatment of those animals."

The Humane Slaughter Act is enforced by the Secretary of Agriculture under provisions of the Federal Meat Inspection Act, 21 U.S.C. §§ 603(b), 610(b), 620(a). The HSA does not apply to chickens or other birds.[17] In 2002, P.L. 107-171, § 10815, 7 U.S.C. § 1907, added a section to the HSA directing the Secretary of Agriculture to submit a report to Congress on practices involving nonambulatory livestock (commonly known as "downed animals"). It also authorized the Secretary, based on the findings of the report, to promulgate regulations to provide for the humane treatment of such animals.[18]

ICCVAM Authorization Act of 2000, 42 U.S.C. §§ 285*l* - 285*l*-6

This statute provides that the Interagency Coordinating Committee on the Validation of Alternative Methods (ICCVAM) shall, among other things, "[r]eview and evaluate new or revised or alternative test methods," and "[f]acilitate appropriate interagency and international harmonization of acute or chronic toxicological test protocols that encourage the reduction, refinement, or replacement of animal test methods."

The ICCVAM was established by the Director of the National Institute of Environmental Health Sciences pursuant to section 463A(b) of the Public Health Services Act (NIEHS), 42 U.S.C. § 285*l*-1(b). The ICCVAM Authorization Act of 2000 requires the Director of the NIEHS to designate the ICCVAM "as a permanent interagency coordinating committee of the Institute [the NIEHS] under the National Toxicology Program Interagency Center for the Evaluation of Alternative Toxicological Methods." The new act also provides that the ICCVAM shall be composed of the heads (or their designees) of 15 named federal agencies plus "[a]ny other agency that develops, or employs tests or test data using animals, or regulates on the basis of the use of animals in toxicity testing."

International Dolphin Conservation Act of 1992, P.L. 102-523

This statute amended the Marine Mammal Protection Act of 1972, the Tuna Conventions Act of 1950, and the South Pacific Tuna Act of 1988, all of which are discussed in this report.

---

[17] Levine v. Conner, 540 F. Supp. 2d 1113 (N.D. Cal. 2008).

[18] The study has not been completed, but USDA has published estimates on the number of nonambulatory cattle, horses, sheep, and goats in the United States. Regulations on nonambulatory cattle are codified at 9 C.F.R. § 309.3(e). For additional information, see CRS Report RS22819, *Nonambulatory Livestock and the Humane Methods of Slaughter Act*, by Geoffrey S. Becker; see also Jennifer L. Mariucci, *The Humane Methods of Slaughter Act: Deficiencies and Proposed Amendments*, 4 Journal of Animal Law 149 (Apr. 2008), at http://www.animallaw.info/journals/jo_pdf/jouranimallawvol4_p149.pdf.

International Dolphin Conservation Program Act, P.L. 105-42 (1997)

This statute amended the Marine Mammal Protection Act of 1972, the Dolphin Protection Consumer Information Act, and the Tuna Conventions Act of 1950, all of which are discussed in this report.[19]

Lacey Act, 18 U.S.C. §§ 41-48 (see also Animal Enterprise Protection Act of 1992, and Depictions of Animal Cruelty)[20]

This statute makes it a crime to (1) willfully disturb or kill any bird, fish, or wild animal, or take or destroy the eggs or nest of any bird or fish, on any lands or waters set apart or reserved under federal law as sanctuaries, refuges, or breeding grounds for such birds, fish, or animals (18 U.S.C. § 41); (2) import species of wild animals, wild birds, fish (including mollusks and crustacea), amphibians, reptiles, or the offspring or eggs or any of the foregoing which the Secretary of the Interior prescribes by regulation to be injurious to human beings or to the interests of agriculture, horticulture, forestry, or wildlife, except that the Secretary may permit importation for zoological, education, medical, or scientific purposes (18 U.S.C. § 42); or (3) use an aircraft or a motor vehicle to hunt, or to pollute a watering hole of, any wild unbranded horse, mare, colt, or burro running at large on any public land or ranges (18 U.S.C. § 47).[21] P.L. 110-161, § 109, 121 Stat. 2119 (2007), contains an exception to this last provision. It permits the Secretary of the Interior to use "helicopters or motor vehicles on the Sheldon and Hart National Wildlife Refuge for the purpose of capturing and transporting horses and burros," but "[s]uch use shall be in accordance with humane procedures prescribed by the Secretary."

Lacey Act Amendments of 1981, 16 U.S.C. §§ 3371-3378

This statute, as amended in 1988, makes it unlawful to engage in commerce in any fish or wildlife or plant taken, possessed, transported, or sold in violation of any treaty, or any federal or state law or regulation, or any Indian tribal law. This statute was amended by the Captive Wildlife Safety Act, P.L. 108-191 (2003), to cover "prohibited wildlife species," which it defines as "any live species of lion, tiger, leopard, cheetah, jaguar, or cougar or any hybrid of such species." The Captive Wildlife Safety Act, however, "does not apply to any licensed, registered, and federally inspected exhibitor (zoos, circuses, etc.) or research facility. It also exempts sanctuaries, humane

---

[19] See, Kristin L. Stewart, *Dolphin-Safe Tuna: The Tide is Changing*, 4 Animal Law 111 (1998).

[20] 18 U.S.C. § 49 provides penalties for violations of the animal fighting prohibitions of the Animal Welfare Act, discussed above.

[21] P.L. 101-647, § 1206(a) (1990), repealed a section of the Lacey Act that protected carrier pigeons owned by the United States or bearing a band owned and issued by the United States. 18 U.S.C. § 45.

societies, animal shelters, or societies for the prevention of cruelty to animals that meet specified criteria."[22]

Magnuson-Stevens Fishery Conservation and Management Act, 16 U.S.C. §§ 1801-1891d

This statute, which was amended by the Magnuson-Stevens Fishery Conservation and Management Reauthorization Act of 2006, P.L. 109-479, provides that, except with respect to highly migratory species of fish, "the United States claims, and will exercise in the manner provided for in this act, sovereign rights and exclusive fishery management authority over all fish, and all Continental Shelf fishery resources. ..." 16 U.S.C. § 1811(a). See also, "Shark Finning Prohibition Act."

Marine Mammal Protection Act of 1972, 16 U.S.C. §§ 1361-1423h

This statute imposes a moratorium on the taking ("take" means "harass, hunt, capture, or kill") and importation of all marine mammals or their products, except that the Secretary of Commerce or Interior (depending on the type of animal) may grant permits to allow taking and importation (1) for scientific research and public display, (2) incidentally, in the course of commercial fishing, and (3) "in accord with sound principles of resource protection and conservation." The act also makes it unlawful, except pursuant to a permit for scientific research, to import a marine mammal that is (1) pregnant, (2) nursing or less than eight months old, (3) taken from a species or population stock designated by the Secretary as depleted, or (4) taken in a manner deemed inhumane by the Secretary.

The act also establishes a Marine Mammal Commission whose duties include undertaking studies and making recommendations as to the protection and conservation of marine mammals. 16 U.S.C. §§ 1401-1402.

An exception to the Marine Mammal Protection Act of 1972 authorizes the Secretary of Defense to "authorize the taking of not more than 25 marine mammals [not a member of an endangered or threatened species] each year for national defense purposes. Any such authorization may be made only with the concurrence of the Secretary of Commerce after consultation with the Marine Mammal Commission. ..." 10 U.S.C. § 7524.

In 1988, P.L. 100-711 added "a number of provisions to the act for the specific purpose of reducing the morality [sic] of porpoise in the course of fishing for yellowfin tuna in the ETP [Eastern Tropical Pacific]."[23]

In 1992, Congress added two new laws to the Marine Mammal Protection Act of 1972. P.L. 102-523 added the International Dolphin Conservation Act of 1992, "to prohibit certain tuna

---

[22] S.Rept. 108-172, 108th Cong., 1st sess. 3 (2003).

[23] H.Rept. 100-970, 100th Cong., 2nd sess. 29 (1988); *reprinted in* 1988 U.S. Code Cong. & Ad. News 6170.

harvesting practices." P.L. 102-587, Title III, added the Marine Mammal Health and Stranding Response Act, which directed the establishment of the Marine Mammal Health and Stranding Response Program, the purpose of which is to collect data on marine mammal health and to coordinate effective responses to unusual mortality events by establishing a process in the Department of Commerce.

The Marine Mammal Protection Act Amendments of 1994, P.L. 103-238, was intended "to improve the program to reduce the incidental taking of marine mammals during the course of commercial fishing operations, and for other purposes. ..." S.Rept. 103-220, 103rd Cong., 2nd sess. (1994). The 1994 statute, among other things, amended 16 U.S.C. § 1374 to authorize the Secretary of Commerce to issue permits "for the importation of polar bear parts (other than internal organs) taken in sport hunts in Canada," but required the Secretary to "undertake a scientific review of the impact of [such] permits ... on the polar bear population stocks in Canada within 2 years. ..." 108 Stat. 539 (1994).

The 1994 statute also amended 16 U.S.C. § 1374 to provide that the Secretary of Commerce may issue permits "to take or import a marine mammal for the purpose of public display only to a person which the Secretary determines ... is registered or holds a license issued under" the Animal Welfare Act. The effect of this provision apparently is that the Department of Agriculture rather than the National Marine Fisheries Service is authorized to regulate such marine mammals once they are held in captivity. 108 Stat. 537 (1994).[24]

In 1997, the International Dolphin Conservation Program Act, P.L. 105-42, amended various provisions of the Marine Mammal Protection Act of 1972. In 2007, title IX of the Magnuson-Stevens Fishery Conservation and Management Reauthorization Act of 2006, P.L. 109-479, added the United States-Russia Polar Bear Conservation and Management Act of 2006 to the Marine Mammal Protection Act of 1972.

Marine Plastic Pollution Research and Control Act of 1987, P.L. 100-220, Title II

This statute amended the act to Prevent Pollution from Ships, 33 U.S.C. §§ 1901-1915, to, among other things, direct the Environmental Protection Agency, in consultation with the Secretary of Commerce, to study "improper disposal practices and associated specific plastic articles that occur in the environment with sufficient frequency to cause death or injury to fish or wildlife."

Marine Protection, Research, And Sanctuaries Act of 1972, 16 U.S.C. §§ 1431-1445b

This statute authorizes the Secretary of Commerce to designate national marine sanctuaries.

---

[24] This provision was opposed by animal rights advocates, who took the position that "NMFS has years of experience in monitoring this act, as well as other marine mammal issues. In contrast, the USDA has lacked both the commitment and ability to protect animals under the federal Animal Welfare Act." Animal Legal Defense Fund, *The Animals' Advocate* (spring 1994) at 2.

Marine Turtle Conservation Act of 2004, 16 U.S.C. §§ 6601-6607

This statute states that its purpose "is to assist in the conservation of marine turtles and the nesting habitats of marine turtles in foreign countries by supporting and providing financial resources for projects to converse the nesting habitats, conserve marine turtles in those habitats, and address other threats to the survival of marine turtles."

Migratory Bird Conservation Act, 16 U.S.C. §§ 715-715s

This statute authorizes the Secretary of the Interior to purchase or rent such areas as have been approved for purchase or rental by the Migratory Bird Conservation Commission "which he determines to be suitable for use as an inviolate sanctuary, or for any other management purpose, for migratory birds."

Multinational Species Conservation Fund, 16 U.S.C. § 4246

This fund was created in 1998 to carry out the African Elephant Conservation Act, the Asian Elephant Conservation Act, and the Rhinoceros and Tiger Conservation Act. Separate accounts in the fund were established as the Neotropical Migratory Bird Conservation Account, and the Great Ape Conservation Fund.

National Agricultural Research, Extension, and Teaching Policy Act of 1977, 7 U.S.C. §§ 3191-3202

This statute is designed to promote "the improved health and productivity of domestic livestock, poultry, aquatic animals, and other income-producing animals that are essential to food supply of the United States and the welfare of producers and consumers of animal products." 7 U.S.C. § 3191, as amended by P.L. 104-127 (1996), § 810. It was amended in 1990 to require the Secretary of Agriculture to commission the National Academy of Sciences "to conduct a study of the delivery system utilized to provide farmers ... and ranchers with animal care and veterinary medical services, including animal drugs." The study shall assess opportunities to, among other things, "advance the well-being and treatment of farm animals." 7 U.S.C. § 3193.[25]

---

[25] This statute also required the Secretary to establish the Animal Health Science Research Advisory Board, which expired September 30, 1995. It was directed to advise the Secretary with respect to the implementation of animal health and disease research programs, and was required to have twelve members, one of whom had to be a "person representing an organization concerned with the general protection and well-being of animals." 7 U.S.C. § 3194.

P.L. 104-127 (1996), § 812, amended 7 U.S.C. § 3196(c) to provide:

> In order to establish a rational allocation of funds appropriated under this section, the Secretary shall establish annual priority lists of animal health and disease, food safety, and animal well-being problems of national or regional significance. ... In establishing such priorities, the Secretary, the Joint Council, the Advisory Board, and the Board shall consider the following factors: ... (3) issues of animal well-being related to production methods that will improve the housing and management of animals to improve the well-being of livestock production species.

National Fish and Wildlife Foundation Establishment Act, 16 U.S.C. §§ 3701-3710

This statute created the National Fish and Wildlife Foundation as a nonprofit corporation to, among other things, "encourage, accept and administer private gifts of property for the benefit of, or in connection with, the activities and services of the United States Fish and Wildlife Service. ..."

National Housing Act, 12 U.S.C. § 1701r-1

A 1983 amendment to this statute prohibits owners or managers of federally assisted rental housing for the elderly or handicapped to (1) as a condition of tenancy or otherwise, prohibit, or prevent tenants from keeping "common household pets," or (2) restrict or discriminate against any person in connection with admission to, or continued occupancy of, such housing by reason of the presence of such pets. The Secretary of Housing and Urban Development and the Secretary of Agriculture are authorized to issue regulations establishing guidelines under which housing owners or managers may prescribe reasonable rules for the keeping of pets, including restricting pet size and types of pets.[26] Owners or managers may require the removal of pets "duly determined" to constitute a nuisance or a threat to health or safety.

P.L. 105-276, § 526 (1998), added a new § 31 to the United States Housing Act of 1937, 42 U.S.C. § 1437z-3, which extended the right to keep common household pets to residents of all public housing, not only to residents of public housing designated for the elderly or handicapped. (The right to keep pets in federally assisted rental housing for the elderly or handicapped remains under the National Housing Act.) The new provision took effect August 9, 2000. 24 C.F.R. Part 960.

National Wildlife Refuge System Administration Act of 1966, 16 U.S.C. §§ 668dd-668ee

This statute established the National Wildlife Refuge System, which is administered by the Secretary of the Interior through the United States Fish and Wildlife Service. The purpose of the

---

[26] Regulations under this section are published at 24 C.F.R. §§ 5.300-5.380.

System is to "consolidat[e] the authorities relating to the various categories of areas that are administered by the Secretary of the Interior for the conservation of fish and wildlife. ..."

Neotropical Migratory Bird Conservation Act, 16 U.S.C. §§ 6101-6109

This statute "established in the Multinational Species Conservation Fund of the Treasury a separate account to be known as the 'Neotropical Migratory Bird Conservation Account.'" The fund is to be used for a program, established by the Secretary of the Interior, "to provide financial assistance for projects to promote the conservation of neotropical migratory birds."

Nonindigenous Aquatic Nuisance Prevention and Control Act of 1990, 16 U.S.C. §§ 4701-4751

This statute is intended "to prevent unintentional introduction and dispersal of nonindigenous species into waters of the United States through ballast water management and other requirements." The statute finds that nonindigenous species, such as the zebra mussel, if left uncontrolled, would disrupt the economy and "the diversity and abundance of native fish."

North Pacific Anadromous Stocks Act of 1992, 16 U.S.C. §§ 5001-5012

This statute authorizes the Secretary of Commerce to enforce the Convention for the Conservation of Anadromous Stocks in the North Pacific Ocean.

Northern Pacific Halibut Act of 1982, 16 U.S.C. §§ 773-773k

This statute authorizes the Secretary of Commerce to enforce the Convention between the United States of America and Canada for the preservation of the Halibut Fishery of the Northern Pacific Ocean and Bering Sea.

Northwest Atlantic Fisheries Convention Act of 1995, 16 U.S.C. §§ 5601-5612

This statute implements the Northwest Atlantic Fisheries Convention.

Pacific Salmon Treaty Act of 1985, 16 U.S.C. §§ 3631-3645

This statute implements a treaty between the United States and Canada, the purposes of which were to "prevent overfishing and provide for optimum production" and to "provide for each Party to receive benefits equivalent to the production of salmon originating in its waters." The act repealed the Sockeye Salmon or Pink Salmon Fishing Act of 1947, formerly 16 U.S.C. §§ 776-776f.

Pacific Whiting Act of 2006, 16 U.S.C. §§ 7001-7010

This statute requires the Secretary of Commerce to

> establish the United States catch level for Pacific whiting according to the standards and procedures of the Agreement [between the Government of the United States and the Government of Canada on Pacific Hake/Whiting] and this [statute] ... rather than under the standards and procedures of the Magnuson-Stevens Fishery Conservation and Management Act (16 U.S.C. 1801 et seq.), except to the extent necessary to address the rebuilding needs of other species.

Partnerships for Wildlife Act, 16 U.S.C. §§ 3741-3744

"The purposes of this title are to establish a partnership among the United States Fish and Wildlife Service, designated State agencies, and private organizations and individuals—(1) to carry out wildlife conservation and appreciation projects. ..." 16 U.S.C. § 3742.

Pets Evacuation and Transportation Standards Act of 2006, 42 U.S.C. §§ 5170b(a)(3)(J), 5196(e)(4), 5196(j)(2), 5196b(g)

This statute (P.L. 109-308) amended the Robert T. Stafford Disaster and Emergency Assistance Act to authorize federal disaster assistance in the "rescue, care, shelter, and essential needs" of "household pets and service animals"; to authorize the Director of the Federal Emergency Management Agency (FEMA) to develop "plans that take into account the needs of individuals with pets and service animals prior to, during, and following a major disaster or emergency"; to authorize the Director of FEMA to "make financial contributions ... to the States and local authorities for animal emergency preparedness purposes, including the procurement, construction, leasing, or renovating of emergency shelter facilities ..."; and to require the Director of FEMA, "[i]n approving standards for State and local emergency preparedness operational plans ... , [to] ensure that such plans take into account the needs of individuals with household pets and service animals prior to, during, and following a major disaster or emergency."

Pittman-Robertson Wildlife Restoration Act, 16 U.S.C. §§ 669-669k

Also known as the "Federal Aid in Wildlife Restoration Act," this statute authorizes the Secretary of the Interior to cooperate with the states, through their respective fish and game departments, in wildlife restoration projects, which are defined as the "selection, restoration, rehabilitation, and improvement of areas of land or water adaptable as feeding, resting, or breeding places for wildlife." This statute was amended by the Wildlife and Sport Fish Restoration Programs Improvement Act of 2000, discussed below.

Public Health Service Act, 42 U.S.C. §§ 283e, 289d

Section 404C of this statute, 42 U.S.C. § 283e, directs the Director of the National Institutes of Health (NIH), by October 1, 1993, to prepare a plan for the NIH to conduct or support research into methods of biomedical research and experimentation that do not require the use of animals, that reduce the number of animals used, that produce less pain and distress in animals used, and that involve the use of marine life other than marine mammals.

Section 495 of this statute, 42 U.S.C. § 289d, directs the Secretary of Health and Human Services, acting through the Director of the NIH, to establish guidelines for research facilities as to the proper care and treatment of animals, including the appropriate use of tranquilizers, analgesics, and the like; but such guidelines may not prescribe methods of research. Entities that conduct biomedical and behavioral research with NIH funds must establish animal care committees which must conduct reviews at least semi-annually and report to the Director of NIH at least annually. If the Director determines that an entity has not been following the guidelines, he must give it an opportunity to take corrective action, and, if it does not, suspend or revoke its grant or contract.[27]

Recreational Hunting Safety and Preservation Act of 1994, 16 U.S.C. §§ 5201-5207

This statute makes it a violation, subject to a civil penalty of up to $10,000, "intentionally to engage in any physical conduct that significantly hinders a lawful hunt ... on Federal lands." The conference report states that, to be a violation, "the conduct must be intentional, and must be done

---

[27] Another section of the act, enacted in 1985 and repealed in 1988, authorized the Secretary to make grants to schools of veterinary medicine for "the development of curricula for training in the care of animals used in research, the treatment of animals while being used in research, and the development of alternatives to the use of animals in research. ..." P.L. 99-129, § 217(e) (1985), 42 U.S.C. § 295g-8(f); recodified by P.L. 99-660, § 601(a) (1986), as 42 U.S.C. § 295g-8(g); repealed by P.L. 100-607, § 613(a) (1988). Yet another section, enacted in 1986 and repealed in 1992, directed the Administrator of the Alcohol, Drug Abuse, and Mental Health Administration to establish guidelines for the following: "(1) The proper care of animals to be used in research conducted by and through agencies of the Administration, (2) The proper treatment of animals while being used in research ... (3) The organization and operation of animal care committee[s] [to assure compliance with the guidelines]." 42 U.S.C. § 290aa-10(a) (P.L. 99-570, § 420 (1986); repealed by P.L. 102-321, § 120(a) (1992)).

---

with the intention of significantly hindering a lawful hunt."[28] The statute also authorizes injunctive relief against violations.

The conference report gives examples of violations of the statute, including "using visual, aural, olfactory, or physical stimuli to affect wildlife behavior." Ibid. This suggests the possibility that a court could construe mere words addressed to a hunter as "physical conduct," if such words affected wildlife behavior (or a hunter's concentration) so as significantly to hinder a hunt. This apparently would not violate the First Amendment's guarantee of freedom of speech, provided that the statute's civil penalty were imposed on the speaker for the effect of the *sound* of his words and not for their content. The statute states that "[t]he term 'conduct' does not include speech protected by the first article of amendment to the Constitution" (the statute does not otherwise define "conduct" or "physical conduct"), but this of course would go without saying, as Congress cannot punish speech that is protected by the First Amendment.

Rehabilitation Act of 1973:
See Americans with Disabilities Act

Rhinoceros and Tiger Conservation Act of 1994, 16 U.S.C. §§ 5301-5306

This statute created the Rhinoceros and Tiger Conservation Fund "to provide financial assistance for projects for the conservation of rhinoceros and tigers."

Salmon and Steelhead Conservation and Enhancement Act of 1980, 16 U.S.C. §§ 3301-3345

This statute authorizes the establishment of a cooperative program involving the United States, the States of Washington and Oregon, and Indian Tribes, to "encourage stability in and promote the economic well being" of commercial fishing through "coordinated research, enhancement, and management of salmon and steelhead resources and habitat."

Shark Finning Prohibition Act, 16 U.S.C. § 1822 note

This statute amended the Magnuson-Stevens Fishery Conservation and Management Act by adding 16 U.S.C. § 1857(1)(P) to make it unlawful "to remove any of the fins of a shark (including the tail) and discard the carcass of the shark at sea." It also requires the Secretary of Commerce, acting through the Secretary of State, to, among other things, "initiate discussions as soon as possible for the purpose of developing bilateral or multilateral agreements with other nations for the prohibition of shark-finning."

---

[28] H.Rept. 103-711, 103rd Cong., 2nd sess. (1994); reprinted in 1994 U.S. Code Cong. & Ad. News 1874.

Sikes Act, 16 U.S.C. §§ 670a-670o

This statute authorizes the Secretary of Defense

> to carry out a program of planning for, and the development, maintenance and coordination of, wildlife, fish, and game conservation and rehabilitation in each military reservation in accordance with a cooperative plan mutually agreed upon by the Secretary of Defense, the Secretary of Interior, and the appropriate State agency designated by the State in which the reservation is located.

South Pacific Tuna Act of 1988, 16 U.S.C. §§ 973-973r

This statute implements the Treaty on Fisheries Between the Governments of Certain Pacific Island States and the Government of the United States, signed April 2, 1987.

Tariff Act of 1930, 19 U.S.C. § 1527

This section of the Tariff Act of 1930 (also known as the "Hawley-Smoot Tariff Act" and the "Smoot-Hawley Act") prohibits the importation into the United States of any wild mammal or bird, alive or dead, or any part of product of any wild mammal or bird, if the laws or regulations of the country where the wild mammal or bird lives restrict its "taking, killing, possession, or exportation to the United States," unless the wild mammal or bird is accompanied by a certification of the U.S. consul that it "has not been acquired or exported in violation of the laws of regulations of such country. ..."

Any mammal or bird, alive or dead, or any part of product thereof, imported into the U.S. in violation of the above shall be subject to seizure and forfeiture under the customs laws. The Tariff Act of 1930 does not apply in the case of (1) articles the importation of which is prohibited by any other law, including 18 U.S.C. § 42(a) (the Lacey Act), (2) articles imported for scientific or educational purposes, or are migratory, or (3) certain migratory game birds.

Tuna Conventions Act of 1950, 16 U.S.C. §§ 951-962

This statute prohibits fishing in violation of any regulation adopted by the Secretary of Commerce pursuant to the Convention for the Establishment of an Inter-American Tropical Tuna Commission, and prohibits commerce in fish taken in violation of such regulations.

Twenty-Eight Hour Law, 49 U.S.C. § 80502

Prior versions of this law were enacted in 1873 (Ch. 252, 42d Cong., 17 Stat. 584, R.S. §§ 4386-4389) and 1906 (Ch. 3594, 59th Cong., 34 Stat. 607). The 1906 law was repealed and reenacted in amended form (but "without substantive change"[29]) in 1994 by P.L. 103-272. (It was previously

---

[29] H.Rept. 103-180, 103rd Cong., 2nd sess. (1994) at 1; reprinted in 1994 U.S. Code Cong. & Ad. News 818.

codified at 45 U.S.C. §§ 71-74.) It is also known as the "Cruelty to Animals Act," the "Live Stock Transportation Act," and the "Food and Rest Law." As amended in 1994, it provides that "a rail carrier, express carrier, or common carrier (except by air or water), a receiver, trustee, or lessee of one of those carriers, or an owner or master of a vessel transporting animals" across state lines, "may not confine animals in a vehicle or vessel for more than 28 consecutive hours without unloading the animals for feeding, water, and rest."

It also provides that "[a]nimals being transported shall be unloaded in a humane way into pens equipped for feeding, water, and rest for at least 5 consecutive hours." The statute "does not apply when animals are transported in a vehicle or vessel in which the animals have food, water, space, and an opportunity for rest."

The 28-hour period is subject to the following exceptions:

> Sheep may be confined for an additional 8 consecutive hours without being unloaded when the 28-hour period of confinement ends at night. Animals may be confined for—(A) more than 28 hours when the animals cannot be unloaded because of accidental or unavoidable causes that could not have been anticipated or avoided when being careful; and (B) 36 consecutive hours when the owner or person having custody of animals being transported requests, in writing and separate from a bill of lading or other rail form, that the 28-hour period be extended to 36 hours.

The Twenty-Eight Hour Law is enforced by the Attorney General, who, "[o]n learning of a violation ... shall bring a civil action" to collect a penalty of at least $100 but not more than $500 for each violation. The statute does not provide for criminal penalties. The statute does not mention any federal agency or official besides the Attorney General, but its 1906 version provided, "It shall be the duty of all U.S. Attorneys to prosecute all violations of this Act reported by the Secretary of Agriculture," and, as noted above, the 1994 amendment was intended to be "without substantive change" to the 1906 version. In addition, in 1963, the USDA issued regulations under the act that remain in effect. 9 C.F.R. §§ 89.1-89.5. Therefore, it appears that the USDA continues to play a role in enforcing the act.

In 2006, noting "that the plain meaning of the statutory term 'vehicle' in the Twenty-Eight Hour Law includes 'trucks' which operate as express carriers or common carriers," the USDA decided for the first time to interpret the act to include the transportation of animals by trucks.[30] In the same document in which it announced this decision, the USDA noted: "The Twenty-Eight Hour Law was never construed as being applicable to poultry, and ... USDA does not intend to change this longstanding interpretation of the statute."

---

[30] Letter from W. Ron DeHaven, Administrator, to Peter A. Brandt, Esq., The Humane Society of the United States (September 22, 2006).

United States Housing Act of 1937: See National Housing Act

United States-Russia Polar Bear Conservation and Management Act of 2006, 16 U.S.C. §§ 1423-1423h

This statute, which is part of the Marine Mammal Protection Act of 1972, makes it unlawful "to take any polar bear in violation of the Agreement [Between the Government of the United States of America and the Government of the Russian Federation on the Conservation and Management of the Alaska-Chukotka Polar Bear Population]." It also makes it unlawful "to import, export, possess, transport, sell, receive, acquire, or purchase, exchange, [or] barter ... any polar bear, or any part or product of a polar bear, that is taken in violation of" the agreement or other restriction that is adopted by the commission established under the agreement. The Secretary of the Interior is authorized to enforce the act.

Wendell H. Ford Aviation Investment and Reform Act for the 21ˢᵗ Century, 49 U.S.C. § 41721

This statute, enacted April 5, 2000, requires air carriers that provide scheduled passenger air transportation to submit monthly reports to the Secretary of Transportation on any incidents involving the loss, injury, or death of an animal. The statute requires the Secretary to publish this data in a manner comparable to other consumer complaint and incident data.

Western and Central Pacific Fisheries Convention Implementation Act, 16 U.S.C. §§ 6901-6910

This statute provides for the representation of the United States on the Commission for the Conservation and Management of Highly Migratory Fish Stocks in the Western and Central Pacific Ocean.

Whale Conservation And Protection Study Act, 16 U.S.C. §§ 917-917d

This statute directs the Secretary of Commerce to "undertake comprehensive studies of all whales found in waters subject to the jurisdiction of the United States."

Whaling Convention Act of 1949, 16 U.S.C. §§ 916-916*l*

This statute prohibits whaling and commerce in whale products in violation of the International Whaling Convention for the Regulation of Whaling or in violation of any regulation of the International Whaling Commission or the Secretary of Commerce.

Wild Bird Conservation Act of 1992, 16 U.S.C. §§ 4901-4916

The purpose of this act is to promote the conservation of exotic birds by assisting wild bird conservation and management programs in the countries of origin of wild birds, and limiting the importation of exotic birds.

Wild Free-Roaming Horses and Burros Act, 16 U.S.C. §§ 1331-1340

This statute makes it a crime, with respect to any wild free-roaming horse or burro, to (1) remove it from the public lands without authority from the Secretary of the Interior or Agriculture (depending on the public land), (2) convert it to private use, without authority from the Secretary, (3) maliciously cause its death or harassment, (4) process its remains into commercial products, or (5) sell it if it is maintained on private or leased land.

Wildlife and Sport Fish Restoration Programs Improvement Act of 2000, 16 U.S.C. §§ 669-669k

This statute amends the Pittman-Robertson Wildlife Restoration Act to authorize firearm and bow hunter education and safety program grants, and to establish a multistate conservation grant program. Grants under the latter may not be used "for an activity, project, or program that promotes or encourages opposition to the regulated hunting or trapping of wildlife" (§ 113).

This statute also amends the Dingell-Johnson Sport Fish Restoration Act to establish a multistate conservation grant program, grants under which may not be used "for an activity, project, or program that promotes or encourages opposition to the regulated taking of fish" (§ 122).

Yukon River Salmon Act of 1995, 16 U.S.C. §§ 5701-5709

This statute implements "the interim agreement for the conservation of salmon stocks originating from the Yukon River in Canada. ..."

Author Contact Information

Vivian S. Chu
Legislative Attorney
vchu@crs.loc.gov, 7-4576

Acknowledgments

Henry Cohen, Legislative Attorney, was the initial author of this report.